Richard Caton

Two Lectures on the Temples and Ritual of Asklepios at Epidaurus

and Athens

Richard Caton

Two Lectures on the Temples and Ritual of Asklepios at Epidaurus and Athens

ISBN/EAN: 9783743441774

Manufactured in Europe, USA, Canada, Australia, Japa

Cover: Foto ©ninafisch / pixelio.de

Manufactured and distributed by brebook publishing software
(www.brebook.com)

Richard Caton

Two Lectures on the Temples and Ritual of Asklepios at Epidaurus

and Athens

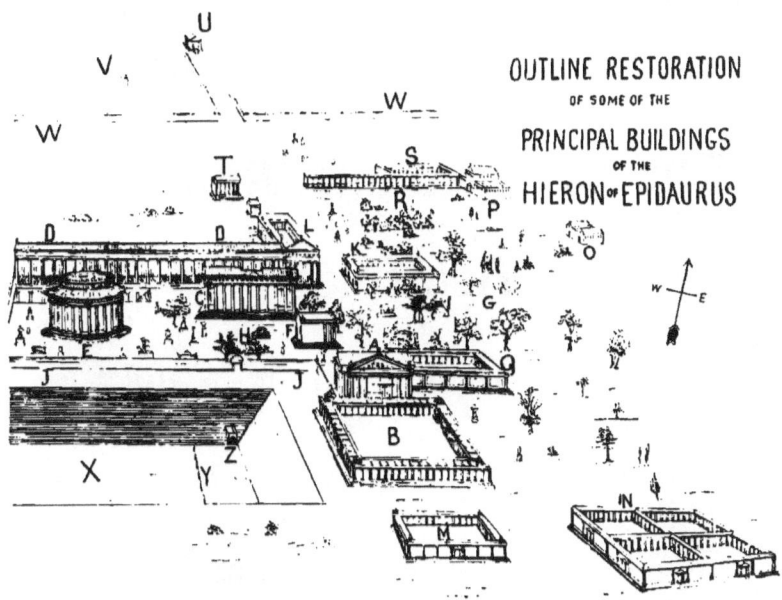

PLATE I.—OUTLINE RESTORATION OF A PART OF THE HIERON OF EPIDAURUS.

A South Propylæa. **B** Gymnasium (?). **C** Temple of Asklepios. **D D** The east and west Abaton; the lower story of the latter and the steps leading down to it are shown. **E** The Tholos. **F** Temple of Artemis. **G** The Grove. **H** Small altar. **I** Large altar (?). **J** South boundary of sacred precinct. **K** The "Square building." **L** The baths of Asklepios. **M** Supposed gymnasium or hostel. **N** The building with four quadrangles. **O** Roman building. **P** Roman baths. **Q** Supposed portico of Cotys. **R** North-eastern Colonnade. **S** North-eastern quadrangle. **T** Supposed temple of Aphrodite. **U** Northern Propylæa on road from town of Epidaurus. **V** Roman building. **W** Northern boundary of precinct. **X** Stadium. **Y** Goal, or perhaps starting-place. **Z** Tunnel communicating with precinct. (R. C.)

TWO LECTURES

ON

The Temples and Ritual of

Asklepios

AT EPIDAURUS AND ATHENS.

DELIVERED AT THE ROYAL INSTITUTION OF GREAT BRITAIN.

BY

RICHARD CATON, M.D., F.R.C.P.

HON. PHYSICIAN LIVERPOOL ROYAL INFIRMARY;
EMERITUS PROFESSOR OF PHYSIOLOGY, UNIVERSITY COLLEGE, LIVERPOOL.

[*Reprinted from* "OTIA MERSEIANA."]

1899.

TWO LECTURES ON THE TEMPLES AND RITUAL OF ASKLEPIOS AT EPIDAURUS AND ATHENS.

Delivered at the Royal Institution of Great Britain.

By RICHARD CATON, M.D., F.R.C.P.

LECTURE I.

LADIES AND GENTLEMEN,

You are aware that during the last twenty-five years the energy and enthusiasm in archæological research of such men as Dr. Schliemann have not merely thrown a considerable amount of light on historic and prehistoric Greece, but have also awakened a keener enthusiasm among classical scholars and in Societies devoted in various countries to archæological investigation. Even Governments have been influenced and induced to help on the progress of these most interesting studies. The German Government has spent large sums in the excavation of Olympia and Pergamus. The French Government has wisely and liberally devoted considerable sums to the excavation of Delphi and to other important works. The Greek Government and the Athenian Archæological Society have expended much money and an infinitude of labour on investigations of the classic wealth of their own land.

In these three instances, although the amount paid is trivial when viewed in the national balance-sheet, its archæological equivalent is great. These three countries have not only made the whole world their debtor by the liberality they have displayed, but each has quickened and stimulated a taste for learning and for art among its own people.

One or two other nationalities have had a share in the progress made, though of a more private and individual kind. The American School has explored the Heræon and certain other classical sites, and lastly our own British School in Athens, whose chief wealth has been the enthusiasm of its members, has done much, when we consider its difficulties, and the lack of the sufficient pecuniary support with which other countries have endowed their representatives.

Although considerable interest is felt by the English public in regard to much of the work just referred to, one important field of investigation has remained almost unknown in this country ; I mean the exploration of the shrines of Asklepios, the god of healing, at Epidaurus and Athens, about which I am to have the honour of speaking to you. As the time allotted is brief, it is needful to avoid all prefatory remarks, and to restrict this paper almost entirely to a consideration of the new discoveries and to inferences from them. As a matter of fact, apart from the Hippocratic writings there is but scant information as to the sanitary and medical aspects of Greek life in ancient literature. Homer and Pindar have brief references to Epidaurus and other sanctuaries of the god ; so also Plato, Hippys of Regium, Strabo, and some of the dramatists, as Aristophanes, also certain of the late Greek writers, especially Pausanias. Under these circumstances most precious are the researches made by the spade.

The pioneer in this inquiry was M. Cavvadias, the eminent archæologist, now Minister of Education in the Greek Government. To him more than to anyone else we owe the important additions lately made to this branch of archæology.

He worked largely in conjunction with the Greek Archæological Society, and was aided by many individual members ; for example, M. Staïs, who did excellent work in deciphering the hundreds of inscriptions which were found—a work of no small difficulty.

Various members of the French School, such as M. Gérard, MM. Defrass and Lechat, and Prof. Reinach : Dr. Dörpfeld, Prof. Furtwängler, Herr Baunack, Dr. Köchler, and others associated with the German School, have had a share in the work or in recording its results.

Comparatively little has been done by the English, and still less has been published in our language. An interesting paper by Professor Percy Gardner, in his *New Chapters in Greek History*, some valuable references by Miss Jane Harrison, the admirable notes in Mr. Fraser's new edition of *Pausanias*, and one or two articles in American journals are among the chief.

For details of the work of the various writers *vide* Bibliography below.

I have to express my acknowledgment to the authorities I have named, but chiefly to M. Cavvadias for his kindness in giving me special facilities in Greece, and for allowing me the use of some of his plates ; also to MM. Defrass and Lechat, who permit me to show you some of their beautiful restorations. Apart from these most of the lantern slides I shall show you were taken by myself on the scene of the various excavations or in Museums.[1]

I. THE HIERON OF EPIDAURUS.

According to tradition, Asklepios, the son of Apollo and Koroni, was born in the Hieron valley, in the Argolic peninsula ; the place-names still preserve the legend ; the hamlet of Koroni commemorates his mother, the hill Titthion owes its name to his having been there suckled by a goat, while on the opposite hill, Kynortion, stood the temple of the Maleatean Apollo.

The Hieron six miles from the town of Epidaurus was the chief seat of the worship of Asklepios, though minor ones existed in Athens, at Delphi, Pergamus, Troezen, Cos, Tricca, and other places.

Here is an outline restoration, Plate I, representing some of the principal buildings in the Hieron.

I must warn the reader that the plan does not profess to be accurate. The structural detail of the buildings is always more or less conjectural ; even their relative size and their distances from one another are only approximately correct. The object of the plan is to give a general idea of the arrangement of the chief buildings hitherto discovered, exclusive of the theatre. (It should be stated here that the numbers which follow refer to the illustrations, while the capital letters correspond with those on Plate I.)

A represents the great ceremonial gateway or Propylæa on the south of the precinct. Its close relation to the quadrangle *B* has caused some observers to suppose it was the entrance to *B* alone, but to the writer that seems improbable.

---

[1] About one-third of the lantern slides are here reproduced.

B is a large quadrangle about 250 feet square, reminding one of the Palæstra at Olympia. The central space was surrounded by small rooms and a colonnade; some of the columns of the latter remain, embedded in the later Roman brickwork of a music-hall or Odeon, constructed within the quadrangle. Nine rows of seats and part of the stage of the Odeon still remain. The building has been supposed to be a gymnasium; but if so, must have ceased to be the scene of gymnastic exercises

PLATE II. – RESTORATION OF PART OF ABATON AND OF TEMPLE OF ASKLEPIOS.
(Defrass.)

after the quadrangle was built upon in Roman times. Was it a hostel?

C represents the Temple of Asklepios, the central shrine, a richly decorated and coloured Doric building, erected in the fourth century B.C., as shown in the accompanying restoration by Defrass, Plate II. At the east and west gables were pediment groups representing a battle with Centaurs and a combat of Greeks and Amazons, Plate IV; together with Acroteria,

Plate III, Nereids alighting from horseback, on the two sides, and a central winged victory. A beautiful ivory door, which cost 3,000 drachmæ, closed the sanctuary; within the cella was a single chamber; there was no opisthodomus. Here stood, as shown in Defrass's drawing Plate V, the great chryselephantine statue of Asklepios made by Thrasymedes of Paros, a work somewhat resembling the Parthenon figure, or the vast Zeus of Olympia; the flesh was ivory, the rest gold splendidly enamelled in colours. The god was sitting on a throne, a large golden

PLATE III.—NEREID.

serpent rising up to his left hand; on his right lay a dog, and in front was an altar.

Gold and ivory must have been beautiful materials for the sculptor, though involving much difficulty when combined. The disappearance of chryselephantine sculpture in modern times is perhaps due to this difficulty in production, but probably more to the fact that the ivory usually tended to crack. The great figure of Athena in the Parthenon needed, we know, to be frequently moistened on its ivory surface with water. At Olympia, oil was

applied to the great figure of Zeus, but curiously enough the
Asklepios at Epidaurus needed neither. As the god of medicine,
it may be supposed that he was able to preserve his own integu-
ment, but Pausanias tells us that a well, beneath the pavement
of the temple, diffused sufficient moisture to prevent contraction
and cracking of the ivory.

Plate VI shows the foundations of the Temple as they now
exist. D D in my first illustration is the Ionic portico or
Abaton, a part of which is seen in the second photograph; the

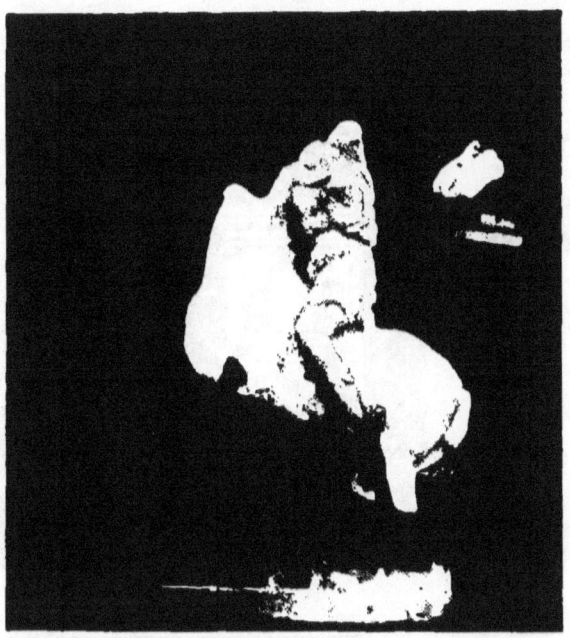

PLATE IV.—AMAZON.

western part is in two storeys, the lower one being in the basement.
It is open on the south side; a double colonnade supports the
roof, the eaves of which, together with the walls and columns,
showed colour decoration. This constituted the ward or sleeping
place for the sick who were awaiting the miraculous inter-
position of the god. The Abaton was furnished with pallets,
lamps, tables, altars, and probably curtains, the patients themselves supplying their own bed clothing. The details of this
building I shall give in my next lecture.

Plate VII shows the remains of the eastern part of the Abaton and Plate VIII the remains of the lower storey of the western part. The latter photograph was taken from the top of the stairs leading down to the area-like court from which access was obtained to the lower storey. *E* in Plate I is the Tholos or Thumela (shown in the annexed restoration by Defrass), Plate IX, the most beautiful circular temple probably that the Greeks ever built, far surpassing the Philippeion at

PLATE V.—RESTORATION OF CHRYSELEPHANTINE FIGURE OF ASKLEPIOS.
(Defrass.)

Olympia. It was built in the fourth century B.C., by Polycleitus the younger, and took twenty-one years to build; externally there was a beautiful Doric colonnade, with peculiarly rich cornice, coloured. Within was a circle of sixteen graceful Corinthian columns of marble, the wall and floor were also decorated with variously coloured marbles. Here were two celebrated paintings by Pausias, the Greek artist; the first represented Methe (drunkenness), a woman holding a large

wine goblet to her lips, the glass of which was so painted that
the face was seen through it.   The second, a picture of Eros
(Love) laying aside his bow and quiver and taking up his lyre.
Perhaps we may suppose that the painter here indicated the
relation of Bacchus and Venus to the ailments which afflict
mankind.   The scourges which we are told the gods make out
of the pleasant vices of men doubtless often brought the
wealthy Greek as a suppliant to Asklepios.

What was the purpose of the Tholos? Defrass and Lechat

PLATE VI.—BASE OF TEMPLE OF ASKLEPIOS.

believe it was a drinking fountain, a sort of pump-room, in
which in old times a healing spring arose ; if so, we can
imagine the gouty Athenian being sent here to drink large
draughts from the holy spring, he envying meanwhile Methe
and her occupation on the wall before him. The foundations
are curious, consisting of a series of circular walls forming a
labyrinth, every part of which must necessarily be traversed by
the explorer seeking the central space (Plate X).

MM. Defrass and Lechat think this singularly constructed
basement was a water cistern from which the 'Pump-room'

above was supplied. The difficulties attending this rather attractive hypothesis are—(*a*) that the word 'Thumela' means a sacrificing place; (*b*) Pausanias speaks of the Tholos and of the Sacred Well as though they were entirely distinct places; (*c*) after careful search I can find no trace of a water conduit; (*d*) the basement space, I may say confidently, was not cemented, either on wall or floor, as it would have been if to hold water. Not improbably the tholos was employed for minor sacrifices, and perhaps the labyrinth below may have been associated with

PLATE VII.—REMAINS OF EAST ABATON.

some mysterious Asklepian rite of which we are now ignorant; or the labyrinth may have been the home of the sacred serpents. We do not quite know what were the domestic economics of these creatures; they, along with the dogs, were the incarnation of the god. They were treated by the sick with the utmost veneration; perhaps this curious basement structure was their retreat, and conceivably the upper stage of the tholos was employed for the offering of sacrifices to them as representatives of the god.

Plate I, Fig. *F*. The Temple of Artemis is smaller than that of Asklepios (see Plate XI); the eaves were decorated by a rich cornice of sculptured heads of dogs, the attribute of Artemis-Hekate. She was a divinity of healing and succour, the chaste moon goddess, and sister of Apollo, who healed Æneas. Acroteria of Victories decorated the western gable; within was a row of marble columns, and externally stood a figure of Artemis-Hekate.

PLATE VIII.—REMAINS OF LOWER STOREY OF WEST ABATON.

Letter *G* in Plate I shows the position of the Grove, which probably extended also in the direction of the Tholos. *H* in the same plate shows the position of an altar which may have been sacred either to Asklepios or to Artemis. The letter *I* shows a foundation on which probably a much larger altar formerly stood; it may have been that of Asklepios on which possibly holocausts were offered. *J* represents the southern boundary of the precinct.

K in Plate I represents the square building which has occasioned much discussion. It contains the base of an altar surrounded by many bones of sacrificial animals and much ash, also fragments of bronze and earthenware, many of them bearing dedications to Apollo or Asklepios. Its period of erection seems to have been not later than the beginning of the fifth century B.C. It contained great numbers of statues and inscriptions. It may have been a large open portico giving shelter to

PLATE IX.—Restoration of Tholos. (Defrass.)

the sick during rain, hot sun, or cold winds; employed also for minor sacrifices and for the exhibition of statuary, ex-votos, and inscriptions. On the other hand, it may have been a house for priests or officials, or even a hostel, or possibly contained the library, the locality of which has not yet been identified.

L in Plate I represents a large building, irregular, and of various date; believed to have been the baths of Asklepios; this building perhaps may have also contained the library, which was dedicated to the Maleatean Apollo, and Asklepios, which one would think is likely to have been in some central position.

M in Plate I is intended to represent a rectangular building of which only small traces remain. Whether or not it was a definitely constructed quadrangle, such as I have drawn, may be uncertain. If it was, perhaps we have here the remains of one of the two gymnasia which the inscriptions tell us existed at the Hieron.

PLATE X.—FOUNDATION OF THOLOS.

N in the same plate is a restoration of the building with the four quadrangles, only lately excavated. It is the largest building yet discovered at the Hieron, being nearly 90 yards square. Each of the four quadrangles is surrounded by a number of rooms. In all there were between seventy and eighty of these apartments, each of which opened into its own quadrangle (so far as I could judge). A colonnade ran round the interior of each quadrangle. Query, what is it?—a gymnasium, a palæstra, a college for the priests, or a great hostel? I confess the last-named seems the most probable. When one considers the large number of the sick who came to the Hieron, it is obvious that extensive accommodation must have been provided for them somewhere. The two chambers of the abaton could not have held more than 120 beds, supposing

PLATE XI.—RESTORATION OF TEMPLE OF ARTEMIS.   (R. C.)

these to have been placed in two rows, or if we suppose the almost dark lower storey of the western end to have been a dormitory also, 180 would then have been the greatest possible accommodation. If this were the extreme number to be entertained, why were seats for 12,000 or 14,000 provided in the Stadium, and why was the great theatre seated for at least 9,000 spectators? It appears likely, therefore, that this and other undetermined buildings were hostels for the accommodation of those whose ailments were slight or who were convalescent.

The remains of this curious structure are shown as seen from a distance in Plate XVI below.

O in Plate I is a small building of the Roman period the purpose of which is undetermined.

P is a building also of the Roman period, and evidently contained baths. There are traces of a hypocaust. The remains

PLATE XII.—NORTH-EASTERN COLONNADE.

of hot-air or hot-water pipes are abundant, and certain curious apse-like recesses in the walls containing a seat and terminating below in a bath or deep bason were evidently a form of sitz-bath. When we remember that the French have lately discovered at Delphi no less than three extensive bathing establishments, adjacent to the walls of the precinct on the east, west, and south sides respectively, it is not surprising that we should find at least two such buildings at Epidaurus.

Q in Plate I, a quadrangular building between the Temple of Artemis and the South Portal. Round three, if not four, of its sides were rooms, as in the case of the great four-quadrangle building; many remains of columns are seen. Its purpose is not known with certainty. It may have been a gymnasium or a hostel, or perhaps it is the Colonnade of Cotys which Pausanias mentions.

PLATE XIII.   FIGURE OF APHRODITE.

This Colonnade of Cotys, we know, was originally built of sun-dried brick, and may perhaps originally have had wooden columns. Sun-dried brick, so common in many parts of Greece to-day, was often used in ancient times for important purposes, as for example in the building of the Heraeon at Olympia. When this somewhat perishable material was covered with a fine hard cement, which resisted the heaviest rain, walls so constructed became wonderfully durable. The Colonnade of

Cotys was rebuilt during Roman times. Some of the roof tiles
discovered lately bear the name of Antoninus.

R in Plate I is a colonnade which extended east and west
nearly at right angles with the Roman baths *P* described above.
Plate XII shows the remains of this colonnade, also a small
open aqueduct with basons in its course about eleven yards
apart. This small water channel reminds the visitor of a
similar one existing in front of the Echo Colonnade at Olympia ;

PLATE XIV.—NORTHERN PROPYLÆA AND WELL.

the latter contains one or two basons like those shown in the
plate. This view shows in the distance the Roman baths (*P*).

Adjoining this colonnade on the north-east is a large
quadrangle *S*, formerly bordered on its four sides by columns.
Its length east and west was about double its breadth north
and south.

T is believed by M. Cavvadias to be the Temple of
Aphrodite, a Doric structure only excavated in 1892. An

inscription discovered on the spot speaks of the sanctuary of Aphrodite; not far from it was found a statue of the goddess in Parian marble, a most beautiful figure now preserved in the Museum at Athens.

Plate XIII is an attempt to represent it.

U in Plate I is an Ionic building the present condition of which is shown in Plate XIV. It may be a temple external to the precinct, or it may, as others suggest, be the Northern

PLATE XV.—THEATRE.

Propylæa or Ceremonial Gateway. *V* is a Roman building of unknown purpose, and *IV* represents a barrier which probably was the northern wall of the precinct.

Plate XV represents a side view of the theatre (which is not shown in the outline plan Plate I).

The Great Theatre situated to the south of the precinct was built about the year 450 B.C. by Polycleitus, the architect of the tholos. Pausanias, who was a great traveller, tells us it

2

was the most interesting of all the theatres existing in his time,
and to-day anyone who is familiar with the theatres of Greece
and the Greek colonies will say that this is more impressive
than any of them.   The Koilon or auditorium consisted of
fifty-five rows of marble seats, with twenty-four lines of stairs.
The space for the chorus is, according to the ancient system,
circular, and in the centre doubtless stood an altar of Bacchus.

PLATE XVI.—VIEW OF THEATRE FROM TOP ROW OF SEATS, RUINS OF THE
"FOUR-QUADRANGLE BUILDING" IN THE DISTANCE.

The stage was elevated nearly 12 feet, the proscenium being
enriched by splendid sculpture.   The acoustics of the theatre are
perfect; a sound little louder than a whisper uttered on the
stage can be heard in every part.   The theatre is so placed on
the slope of Kynortion that the occupants of the major part of
the auditorium had a charming view (over the top of the stage)
of the mountains to the north and of the whole range of
beautiful buildings of the Hieron.

Plate XVI represents the view taken from the top row of seats. Note the circular chorus space, the remains of the "four-quadrangle building" and glimpses of the Hieron beyond. While witnessing here the sublime tragedies of Æschylus or Sophocles, or such a comedy as *The Plutus* of Aristophanes (in which, as you will remember, great fun is made of Asklepios and his priests), the contrast afforded by glancing from the stage to the blues and purples of the mountains, the verdancy of the grove,

PLATE XVII.—EAST END OF STADIUM.

and the beautiful forms and colours of the group of temples would be most pleasing. The Greeks were acute in perceiving and taking advances of subtle sources of pleasure like this, and I believe that the sites of many of their theatres were chosen so as to secure for the audience this double pleasure. The Theatre of Delphi is an example of this provision, as also in a less degree is that of Tauromena. This theatre has been said to seat 12,000 spectators; according to my own rough computation, it unquestionably will hold over 9,000 without crowding.

X in Plate I represents part of the Stadium, which is about six hundred feet long. Here are remains of at least fifteen rows of marble seats. Probably foot races took place here as well as other forms of athletic exercise. All the maps of the Hieron represent the eastern end of the Stadium as semicircular, but so far as one can judge, the latest excavations indicate that it was square, and therefore I have so represented it.

Assuming that the fifteen rows of seats extended from end to end on each side, and allowing a foot and a half for each person, the Stadium would seat twelve thousand spectators on its two sides without computing the seats at the ends.

Plate XVII represents the excavations at the end adjacent to the Hieron. V in Plate I (shown also in Plate XVII) is either the starting-place or the goal. Z is a subterranean passage communicating with the precinct.

An inscription (found in 1896) mentioned by Mr. Fraser, shows that a hippodrome also existed at the Hieron.

On Mount Kynortion, some distance south of the great theatre, stood the temple of the Maleatean Apollo. The remains are so fragmentary that it is difficult to devise a conjectural restoration.

PLATE XVIII.—Portico of Eumenes and Acropolis.

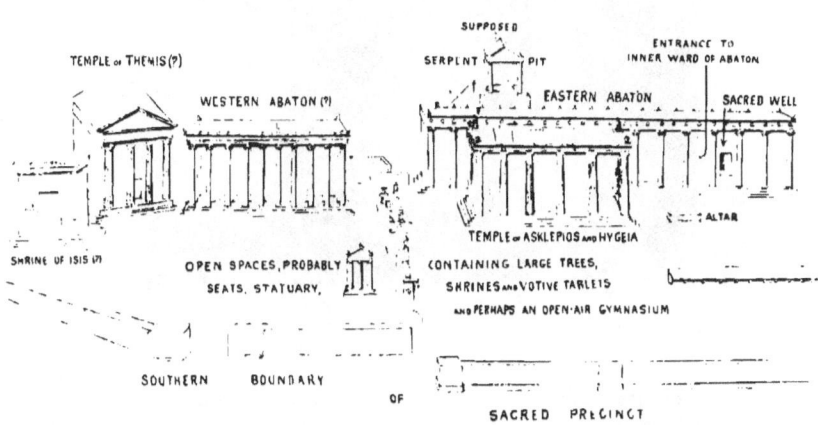

TEMPLE of THEMIS (?)

WESTERN ABATON (?)

SUPPOSED
SERPENT PIT

EASTERN ABATON

ENTRANCE TO
INNER WARD OF ABATON

SACRED WELL

SHRINE OF ISIS (?)

OPEN SPACES, PROBABLY
SEATS, STATUARY,

TEMPLE of ASKLEPIOS and HYGEIA

ALTAR

CONTAINING LARGE TREES,
SHRINES and VOTIVE TABLETS
and PERHAPS AN OPEN-AIR GYMNASIUM

SOUTHERN   BOUNDARY

OF

SACRED   PRECINCT

PLATE XIX.—Attempt at an Outline Restoration of the Asklepieion at
Athens. (R. C.)

II. THE ASKLEPIEION AT ATHENS.

Before saying anything about the ritual and the treatment of the sick at the Hieron, it will be well to turn to the Asklepieion at Athens, and examine briefly the structural arrangements there. Situated on the south side of the Acropolis, at an elevation of

PLATE XX.—REMAINS OF ASKLEPIEION FROM THE WEST.

perhaps eighty feet above the plain, adjoining on the east the theatre of Dionysius, the locality was probably as healthy as any the immediate neighbourhood of Athens could supply.

Plate XVIII represents the remains of the Stoa or Portico of Eumenes (so called) lying to the south of the Acropolis. To the extreme left is seen the Temple of the Nike Apteros and on

the summit of the Acropolis the Parthenon. Between the Stoa
and the rock of the Acropolis is situated the Asklepieion. The
accompanying outline plan, No. XIX, is an attempt to give
some idea of the arrangement of buildings within the precinct.
The buildings were to a certain extent an imitation, on a smaller
scale, and on a limited area, of those at the Hieron of Epidaurus.
Remains of what were probably a temple of Asklepios and
Hygeia, of Doric architecture, also a supposed temple of Themis,

PLATE XXI.--REMAINS OF ASKLEPIEION FROM THE EAST.

and a shrine of Isis, exist, while smaller shrines of Serapis,
Core, Hypnos, Herakles, Panaceia, Demeter, and other divinities
have left no distinct traces. There are considerable remains of
a large eastern portico or abaton of Pentellic marble, from
which is reached a circular chamber in the rock containing the
sacred well.

Plate XX represents the Asklepieion as seen from the
western end and Plate XXI from the east. The building

inscribed "western abaton" in Plan No. XIX may have been a supplementary abaton or a priest's house or a covered gymnasium. A grove existed, perhaps occupying the space between the Stoa of Eumenes and the temples or situated in a large vacant space to the west.

On an elevation above and close to the abaton is a curious well-like structure, surrounded by marble columns, which perhaps was the serpent pit.

PLATE XXII.—Supposed Serpent Pit and remains of Marble Columns round it.

Plate No. XXII represents the remains of this curious and mysterious structure. I have endeavoured to trace a direct communication between this supposed snake pit and the Abaton, but failed to do so.

The grove contained great numbers of statues, busts, ex-votos, and inscriptions. The theatre of Dionysius close at hand was doubtless frequented by the sick as a diversion. The stall occupied by the priest, with his name on it, is still in excellent preservation as seen in Plate XXIII.   He sat in the first rank, with his back to the setting sun, next to the priest of the Muses. The Panathenaic stadium, about half a mile away, doubtless was also frequently visited by the convalescents from the Asklepieion.

PLATE XXIII.—SEATS OF PRIESTS OF ASKLEPIOS AND OF THE
MUSES IN THE THEATRE.

LECTURE   II.

WE now pass on to consider the ritual of the Asklepian shrines and the accommodation and treatment of the sick who frequented them.

It is convenient, first, to consider the Hierarchy.   They consisted of the Hiereus or Hierophant, the priest, who was the head official.   He was appointed annually, and he appears to have been frequently re-elected.   From the Athenian inscriptions we know that sometimes he was a physician, sometimes not; so also it was with the subordinate officials.   The priest was the general administrator, and had a share in the financial government of the temple.   The Dadouchoi, or torch-bearers, were probably subordinate priests; the Pyrophoroi, or fire-carriers, among other functions, lighted the sacred fire on the altars; the Nakoroi or Zakoroi, whose duties in the temple are doubtful, but who sometimes were physicians; the Kleidouchoi, or key-bearers, who perhaps were originally a class of superior door porters, but who appear later to have assumed priestly functions; the Hieromnemones seem to have had purely secular duties, and in common with the Hiereus had charge of all receipts and payments; all were under the rule of the Boule of Epidaurus.   The Kaniphoroi (or basket-bearers) and the Arrephoroi (or carriers of mysteries or holy things) were priestesses. We read in some of the inscriptions of servants or attendants, who ministered to the sick, and carried those who were unable to walk.   Did these women in any degree act as nurses?   It is possible, but no definite information on the subject is given.

There was also a special religious society termed the Asklepiastes.

Turning now from the priests to the suppliants: these, we find, came from all parts of the Greek world, and from what ancient writers tell us, their numbers were great.   Where were they housed?   Some, of course, dwelt in the abaton, the women

probably in one part and the men in another, but, as I have
already pointed out, not more than 120 could find beds there
at a time; perhaps the invalid was only housed there at first,
and when he began to improve was drafted off to a hostel.
Assuming that all the buildings which I have suggested to be
hostels were such, they could not accommodate more than some
four or five hundred patients. Perhaps the usual number attending
may have been only some five or six hundred, while at the great
festivals many thousands assembled. Whether this large number
were lodged in tents or temporary wooden buildings is uncertain.

Probably multitudes of vigorous and able-bodied persons
came to the festivals, and many of them may have been lodged
six miles away at the town of Epidaurus, or in villages or
hamlets adjacent. The ten or twelve thousand who filled the
Theatre or the Stadium cannot have been exclusively sick people.
It seems probable that numbers of athletes and multitudes of
Greeks who merely wanted a holiday and a little excitement
came to the Megala Asklepeia as they came to the Isthmian
or the Olympic games. Setting aside, therefore, all visitors
of this class, who probably brought gains to the Sanctuary,
and for whom accordingly space was provided in the Theatre,
Stadium, and Hippodrome, I pass on to consider the suppliants
proper.

The patient on arriving probably had an interview with the
priest or other official, and arranged about his accommodation
with one of the Hieromnemones, or other secular person. He
performs certain rites, bathes in the sacred fountain, and offers
sacrifices under the direction of the Pyrophorus; the poor man
gives his cake, the rich his sheep or pig, or goat. The votive
tablets frequently show the cakes (πόπανα) being presented, or
sheep, pig, or other animal. Where the ceremonial purification
took place is uncertain. A deep well exists in the eastern
abaton. A stone dropped, struck the water in a fraction over
three seconds, as I found after repeated trials. The well is
therefore over 144 feet deep. Possibly the water used in the
ritual was derived hence, but perhaps the place of purification
has yet to be found. "Only pure souls may enter here," was
inscribed over the entrance of the Asklepian temple.

When night comes the sick man brings his bed clothing
into the abaton, and reposes on his pallet, putting usually some
small gift on the table or altar. The Nakoroi having come round

to light the sacred lamps, the priest enters and recites the evening
prayers to the god, entreating divine help and divine enlighten-
ment for all the sick assembled there; he then collects the gifts
which had been deposited on altars and tables; later the Nakoroi
enter, put out the lights, enjoin silence, and command everyone
to fall asleep and to hope for guiding visions from the god. The
abaton was a lofty and airy sleeping chamber, its southern side
being an open colonnade. It is singularly like the 'shelter
balcony,' or *Liegenhalle*, now used in treating phthisis. This
provision of abundance of pure fresh air for the sick by day and
night, which is so beneficial now, was undoubtedly so then also,
and probably brought much credit to the god and his shrine.

According to the inscriptions the god frequently appeared in
person, or in visions, speaking to the sick man or woman concerning their ailments. Whether these visitations were merely
hallucinations in individuals whose imaginations had been ex-
cited, or whether some priest in the dim light acted the part
of Asklepios; whether the patient was put under the influence
of opium or some other drug provocative of dreams, or whether,
by some acoustic trick, the priests caused the sick to hear spoken
words which they attributed to the deity, it is difficult now to say.

In the accompanying sketch of the abaton a miracle is in
progress in the foreground. A lame man comes to the altar, he
offers his sacrifice, the Pyrophorus lights the sacred flame, the
Dadouchos or Nakoros enjoins silence while the holy serpent
licks the affected part. The abaton is nearly empty, as it is
the daytime, but one or two bedridden patients watch the miracle
with interest.

The valley of the Hieron was the habitat of a large yellow
serpent, perfectly harmless, and susceptible, like most snakes, of
domestication. I am afraid it is now extinct, though it has been
seen during the present century. A number of these creatures
dwelt in the sanctuary, perhaps in the vaults of the tholos. They
were reverenced as the incarnation of the god. The sick were
delighted and encouraged when one of these creatures approached
them; and were in the habit of feeding them with cakes. The
serpents seem to have been trained to lick with their forked tongue
any ailing part. The dog also was sacred to Asklepios, and the
temple dogs in like manner were trained to lick any injured or
painful region of the body.

It will be remembered that in the " Plutus " of Aristophanes, the blind Plutus enters the abaton of the Asklepicion at Athens in order to be cured. Asklepios with his daughters, Iaso and Panaccia, appear in person; they whistle to the sacred serpents, which at once approach, lick the blind eyes, and vision is restored.

PLATE XXIV.
RESTORATION OF THE INTERIOR OF THE ABATON AT EPIDAURUS.
PATIENT SACRIFICING AND HAVING INJURED LEG LICKED BY THE SACRED SERPENT.

In the inscriptions the phrase "ἰάσατο τῇ γλώσσᾳ," referring to the serpent, is common, and also in reference to the dogs " κυὼν τῶν ἱαρῶν ἐθεράπευσε τῇ γλώσσᾳ."

Many of the *malades imaginaires*, who to this day are the
support of the quack, and a cause of embarrassment and difficulty
to the scientific physician, who desires above all things to be
honest, doubtless visited Epidaurus.

The priest would take such a person (as probably he took
all suppliants) into the temple, and cause him to present himself
before the image of the god; prayers, sacrifices, and rites of an
impressive kind were then enacted. Hymns and pæans were
sung to the music of the double flute. The sick man was caused

PLATE XXV.—HEAD OF ASKLEPIOS.

to lay his hand solemnly and reverently on the altar, and then
on the part affected; if there were really nothing the matter, he
was proclaimed to be miraculously cured by the god, and doubtless
his imagination was so impressed that he often himself believed
in the cure.

If the patient were young, sacrifices were doubtless offered at
the shrine of Artemis-Hekate, and perhaps in all cases the pro-
cession of priests and suppliants visited the Tholos and offered

sacrifices there to the god of healing, or ascended Mount Kynortion to the shrine of the great Apollo.

The suppliants spent the day in rest or exercise, as was most agreeable to them. It must be remembered that the precinct was as beautiful as the noblest works of Greek art could make it ; moreover, large and lofty trees formed a shady grove, protecting from the sun heat, while the soft breezes and the sweet pure air of the mountains formed in themselves a potent agency for the restoration of health. The patient had much around

PLATE XXVI.—ASKLEPIOS WITH SERPENT.

him to please and interest—beautiful buildings, rich with sculpture and with colour, scores of statuary figures and groups representing Asklepios and other divinities or subjects from the old Greek mythology in marble and bronze.

Plate XXV represents a head of Asklepios (from the Asklepieion at the Piraeus), to which the genius of the sculptor has given an expression of sorrow and sympathy, as though the god were grieving over the sufferings of mankind.

Plate XXVI shows a full-length figure of the god, found at Epidaurus, accompanied as usual by the serpent. Artistic reliefs, busts, and full - length figures of noted priests and physicians, ex-votos, stelæ, and tablets recording the marvellous cures effected by the god, coloured bas-reliefs, encaustic paintings, shrines, exedræ, decorative vases and fountains, beautified and added interest to the precinct.

Shelter-seats, arranged in semicircles, of beautiful white marble, were so placed as to avoid sun or wind ; they were convenient for converse, or for listening to a reader or a musician.

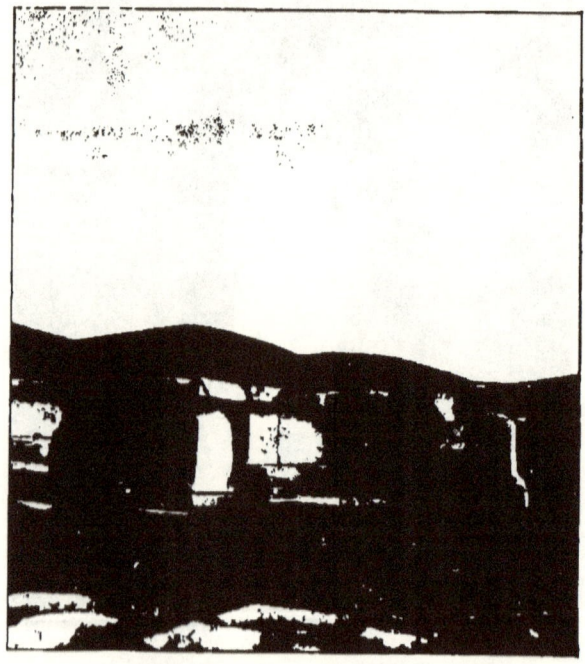

PLATE XXVII.—SHELTER-SEAT.

Plates XXVII and XXVIII represent the remains of two of these seats at the Hieron ; close to the former is seen a large pedestal on which probably an equestrian statue formerly stood.

Many shrines and chapels to subsidiary deities existed, as, for example, to Hygeia, Themis, the Egyptian Apollo, Helios, Selene, Epione (the wife of Asklepios), Zeus, Poseidon, Minerva, Hera, Demeter, and other Eleusinian deities, Dikaiosunae, Telesphorus, Lato, Hypnos, and others not as yet identified.

Plate XXIX represents a number of small figures of Hygeia and of Asklepios from the Hieron.

Every devout Greek who came as a suppliant to Asklepios would find here also a shrine of his own favourite deity.

Those of the sick who were not too ill, would ascend the hill of Kynortion to visit the temple of Apollo, or climb the neighbouring hill of Titthion, sacred to the infancy of Asklepios. Others would engage in the exercises of the gymnasium or the stadium; if unable to participate in these more active pursuits,

PLATE XXVIII.—SHELTER-SEAT.

they would become spectators of them. The plays in the theatre would often make half a day pass pleasantly. We know that both priest and patient went there constantly. Music, religious dances, processions, and festivals would vary the interest and occupations of the day. The studious man could occupy himself with manuscripts from the library, and, reposing in the shelter-seats, would dream over history, plays, or poetry. The solemn rites of the temple, the sacrifices, the study of the multitudinous tablets would all tend to a calm and hopeful condition of mind, eminently helpful to recovery from slight forms of illness, even though no direct medical treatment were pursued.

In earlier times it seems as though the health-restoring influence of the shrines was thought to be wholly miraculous, with but small aid or none from art; the god alone achieved all. The more ancient inscriptions contain childishly absurd reports of miraculous cures.

The ruling idea was that the deity appeared to the sick man in the abaton, applied some medicament, performed some

PLATE XXIX.— FIGURES OF ASKLEPIOS AND HYGIA.

operation, or instructed the dreaming patient to perform some act when he awoke. The frauds of the god or his priest were so outrageous that some of the old Greeks must have been almost as foolish and credulous as many moderns are, who willingly buy soap or pills on no other warranty than the advertisements of the lying and interested vendor.

On the walls of the eastern abaton were fixed two large stone tablets, bearing the title, "Cures by Apollo and Asklepios." Most of the fragments of these tablets have been recovered,

pieced together, and deciphered by M. Staïs and others. The
following are a few extracts :—

Line 72 of the first tablet in the abaton.—A man who had
only one eye is visited by the god in the abaton during the
night. The god applies an ointment to the empty orbit. On
awaking, the man finds he has two sound eyes.

Line 125.—Thyson of Hermione is blind of both eyes ; a
temple dog licks the organs and he immediately regains his sight.

PLATE XXX.—THE STONE MIRACULOUSLY CARRIED BY THE
PARALYZED HERMODIUS.

Line 107.—Hermodius of Lampsacus comes to the Hieron
in a paralyzed condition. As he sleeps in the abaton the god
tells him to rise, to walk outside the precinct, and carry back
into it the largest stone he can find. He does so, and brings
in a stone so heavy that no other man can lift it, and the
stone, as the inscription says, still lies before the abaton. It
lies there to-day, and the visitor may yet in vain emulate the
feat of Hermodius. It will be recognized in the illustration, Plate
XXX, by the hole cut in it to put the hands in.

Line 113.—A man had his foot lacerated by the bite of a wild beast; he is in much pain; the servants of the abaton carry him outside during the daytime; as he is waiting to be healed a serpent follows him, licks his foot, and he is at once cured.

Line 122.—Heræeus of Mytilene has no hair on his head; he asks the god to make it grow again. Asklepios applies an ointment, and next morning the hair has grown thickly over his scalp. (Unfortunately Asklepios forgot to write down the prescription for the benefit of future sufferers from the same defect!)

At line 48 begins a story containing a moral which the priests may have thought it desirable to impress upon their visitors:—

Pandarus comes all the way from Thessaly in order to have a disfiguring eruption or branding mark on his forehead cured; he is quickly made well. Returning to Thessaly his cure is observed by his neighbour Echedorus, who has a similar, but slighter, eruption on the face. He also goes to Hieron, carrying with him a sum of money sent to the god by the grateful Pandarus. Echedorus decides to retain this money himself; he consults the god about his own case, and in answer to a question states that he has brought no gift from Pandarus. On rising in the morning he finds that, instead of having his skin disease cured, that of Pandarus has been added to it.

Line 96.—A man from Toronœa is so unfortunate as to have a stepmother who is not fond of him; she introduces a number of leeches into the wine he drinks. Being of a confiding temperament he swallows them unsuspectingly, but the results are so serious that he is obliged to visit the god. Asklepios cuts open his chest with a knife, removes the leeches, sews up the chest again, and the patient returns home next day.

From other inscriptions we find that Asklepios treats dropsy surgically, in a heroic manner; he first cuts off the patient's head, then holds him up by the heels; the fluid all runs out. He then puts the patient's head on again, and all ends happily.

These, I think, are a sufficient sample of the preposterous stories of cures which the god was reported to have performed in early times.

It is quite clear that the liking which many men and women have for the charlatan, and for deception, their appetites for the marvellous and incredible in all medical matters, existed as strongly among the Greeks as among ourselves, though the superstitious beliefs and the ignorance of science prevailing in those times rendered such folly more excusable than it is now.

In later times it seems clear that superstition and deception had a less share, and art a larger one, in the work of healing at Hieron. Probably among the acute citizens of Athens, at no period were the frauds of the god so outrageous as in the early times at Hieron. We find the priests prescribing many things that were prudent and judicious ; plain and simple diet, hot and cold baths, poulticing for certain chest ailments, and a variety of medicaments—hemlock juice, hellebore, squills, lime-water, and drugs for the allaying of pain—are incidentally mentioned. Water was used extensively both internally and externally, active gymnastic exercise, riding, friction of the skin, massage, and counter-irritation.

The tablet of Apellas of Idria tells us that when visiting the Hieron on account of frequent illness and severe indigestion, the god or his priests ordered a diet of bread and curdled milk, with parsley and lettuce, lemons boiled in water, also milk and honey. Apellas being an irascible person, the god ordered careful avoidance of the emotion of anger, and desired him to run and swing in the gymnasium, and use vigorous friction and counter-irritation to the surface of the body. Probably Apellas was a wealthy and luxurious city-dweller, who took too much food and Chian wine, and who suffered, as many in that age did, from gout. He is eventually cured, and erects a tablet to show his gratitude. .

Here is the thanksgiving of another sufferer : " O blessed Asklepios, God of Healing, it is thanks to thy skill that Diophantes, relieved of his incurable and horrible gout, no longer moves like a crab, no longer will walk upon thorns, but has a sound foot as thou hast decreed."

There can be little doubt that many of the sick benefited greatly by the rest, the pure air, the simple diet, the sources of mental interest, the baths, exercise, massage, and friction, and in later days by the actual medical treatment adopted. Surgical treatment was also employed, for we find marble reliefs of surgical instruments.

Not infrequently it would happen that persons with real and incurable diseases came to Hieron and got worse, notwithstanding their sacrifices and petitions to the god. How the priests excused the impotency of their deity on these occasions we do not know ; perhaps some lack of merit, purity, or sanctity in the individual may have been imputed. We know that in some cases, the honour of Asklepios was saved by sending the unfortunate invalid to some distant shrine ; but of course it happened that in some instances the patient died. Now, according to the religion of the Greeks, two events were considered to desecrate in the most dreadful manner any hallowed precinct—namely, birth and death ; neither of these must occur within any sacred enclosure.

While there was probably much kindliness, humanity, and real help for the sick at these shrines, and much actual benefit resulted, notwithstanding the superstition on which all was based, still, in this one respect, Greek tradition and ceremonial were a cause of the most gross inhumanity. The unhappy visitant whose vital powers were finally declining was received and domiciled in the abaton, but when he failed to improve and was seen by the priests and attendants to be obviously dying, instead of being tenderly nursed and soothed, he was removed from his couch, dragged across the precinct to the nearest gate, expelled, and left to die on the hillside unhelped and untended. Asklepios had rejected him, and no priests or minister of the god must defile himself by any dealings with death. One cannot but hope that the sympathy and humanity which exist naturally in the hearts of most men and all women, found some means of helping these unhappy beings, and that when death seemed probable such sufferers were conveyed to a hostel outside the precinct, and allowed to die in peace there. A like superstition existed regarding birth. Many a poor woman, who was antici- pating maternity and who had been hoping for relief from some ordinary ailment, was suddenly and mercilessly expelled from the precinct just when she needed help and comfort most.

Not until the time of the Antonines was any definite pro- vision made for these two classes of sufferers. Either Antoninus Pius or Marcus Aurelius erected a home for the dying, and a sort of maternity hospital. Doubtless some of the ruins dating from the Roman period, which are at present unidentified, subserved these two purposes.

Among the hundreds of inscriptions found I have thus far only mentioned one class—namely, those referring to cures. There are, in addition, no fewer than thirteen other kinds of inscriptions ; for example, the great poem of Isyllos, describing the genealogy and miracles of Asklepios, written by command of the oracle of Delphi. (The Delphic Sibyl had apparently a great respect for the god of healing. On one occasion she addresses him thus: " O thou who art born to be the World's great joy —.")

Many of the inscriptions are in honour of individual priests, Pyrophori, Hieromnemones, or of distinguished Greeks unconnected with the sanctuaries; for example, there was found in association with a headless statue, the inscription shown below.

Plate XXXI. The upper four lines of the inscription are in the Dorian dialect, the remainder in the Ionian. The former is the dedication of the statue by the Epidaurians to a historian previously unknown to the classical student, a certain Phillipos of Pergamus. The lower Ionic fragment is probably a quotation (the only one known to exist) from his writings.

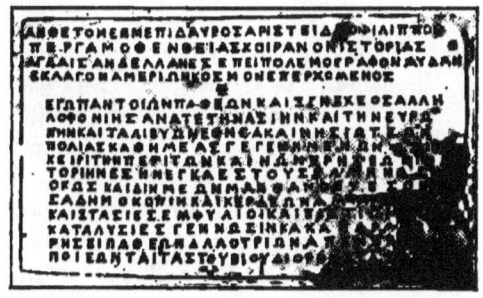

PLATE XXXI.—DEDICATION OF STATUE TO PHILLIPOS.

A learned Oxford friend, whose name I may not disclose, has, with great kindness, edited this inscription for me, supplying the lost words or letters and giving a translation, as follows :—

" ἄνθετο μέν μ' Ἐπίδαυρος Ἀριστείδαο Φίλιππον
Περγάμοθεν Θείας κοίρανον ἱστορίας
ἀγλάϊσαν δ' Ἕλλανες ἐπεὶ πολεμόγραφον, αὐδὰν
ἔκλαγον ἀμερίων κόσμον ἐπερχόμενος.

*   *   *   *

ἐγὼ παντοίων παθέων καὶ συνεχέος ἀλλη-
-λοφονίης ἀνά τέ τὴν Ἀσίην καὶ τὴν Εὐρω-
-πην καὶ τὰ Λιβύων ἔθνεα καὶ νησιωτέων
πόλιας καθ' ἡμέας γεγενημένων ὁσίη

χειρὶ τὴν περὶ τῶν καινῶν πρήξεων ἱσ-
-τοριήν ἐξήνεγκα ἐς τοὺς "Ελληνας
ὅκως καὶ δί ἡμέων μανθάνοντες ὅκο-
-σα δημοκοπίη καὶ κερδέων ἀμ(ετρίαι)
καὶ στάσιες ἐμφύλιοι καὶ πιστίω(ν)
καταλύσιες γεννῶσιν κακὰ παρὰ (τῇ)
ῥήσει παθέων ἀλλοτρίων ἀπενθή(τως)
πὸιεωνται τὰς τοῦ βίου διορθώσιας."

ENGLISH VERSION.

" Set up in stone by Epidauros see,
A peerless scribe of God-like history,
Philip, the son of Aristeidos, come
Unto this holy place from Pergamum :
War was too long the theme of Greece ; my pen
Shrilled to ensue a peace for mortal men.

* * * *

" All sorts of suffering and endless bloodshed having taken
place recently throughout Asia, Europe, the Libyan hordes, the
island cities, I publish to the Greek world, without breach of
trust, a 'History of our own Times,' in order that my countrymen
may learn, by my means, what hosts of evils arise from political
charlatanry and financial greed, quarrels in a nation, and acts
of treachery, and so, by the recital of other people's miseries,
may, without pain or grief to themselves, put their own lives
in order, as occasions arise."

It is somewhat interesting to find the Boule of Epidaurus
thus honouring a historian, and at the same time warning the
Greek people against those political faults to which the nation was
specially prone.

A number of the later inscriptions are in honour of distinguished Romans.

There are numerous inscriptions referring to laws, or judicial
decrees. Others, again, refer to the contests of the Stadium,
while another and especially voluminous class relates to the
construction of the temples and other buildings. In addition
to the names of the architects and contractors, and the
sums paid, these records contain many interesting details, e.g.,
the statement that the pediment groups and acroteria on the
temple of Asklepios were cut in marble by Hektoridas and

another artificer, from models designed by the great sculptor
Timotheus, the artist who, along with Scopas, designed the
Mausoleum of Halicarnassus.

The minute details concerning the building of the tholos, the
amounts paid for marble and other materials, the names of
architects and contractors, the report of the commissioners who
inspected the work, and who formed a sort of lay building com-
mittee; their journeys to Athens, Corinth, Megara, and other
places in quest of material, workmen, etc., the exact sums

PLATE XXXII.—GROUP OF SUPPLIANTS APPROACHING ASKLEPIOS AND HIS FAMILY.

expended on these journeys, and other details, are curious and
interesting. One can only regret that no hint is given of the
use and purpose of the building on which so much care and
thought were expended.

I might occupy much time in showing and describing the
scores of sculptured votive tablets which have been recovered. In
most, of course, the figure of Asklepios has been destroyed or
damaged by the iconoclastic zeal of the early Christian.

In Plate XXXII an almost uninjured example is shown. A group of four suppliants with their children approach the god, who leans on his staff with entwining serpent. Behind Asklepios is seen the head of (probably) his wife Epione, then come Machaon and Podalirius, his sons, then, probably, Hygeia, Panaceia, and Iaso, his daughters. The whole Asklepian family are of heroic stature.

Every fourth year a great festival was held at the Hieron, the Megala Asklepieia, at which athletic contests, races, processions, music, plays in the theatre, holy (perhaps also unholy!) vigils, lasting all night, gorgeous rites, sacrifices, decoration of the temples and precincts, together with feasts, took place. Most probably the priests would arrange for the performance of a few miracles. Other festivals were also held, as the Megala Apolloneia.

On these occasions, if not at other times, doubtless every seat in the theatre, stadium, and hippodrome would be filled, mostly by sound and healthy visitors, coming, as I have suggested above, partly to enjoy a holiday, partly to witness athletic exercises, which interested them quite as much as important cricket, football, or rowing contests interest us, and partly to do honour to the god whose aid they might need when sickness or old age should enfeeble them.

Lastly, there is a link which, though of no practical import, is still a genuine historic bond connecting the Hieron of Epidaurus with the medicine of Western Europe. Three centuries B.C. Rome was visited by dire pestilence. The rulers of Rome, having in vain endeavoured to check it, sought the counsel of the Sibylline books, and were directed to bring Asklepios to Rome from Epidaurus. A galley was sent to the Saronic Gulf, and a mission visited the Hieron, bringing back to the ship one of the sacred serpents. The galley returned, entered the Tiber, approached Rome, and as it touched the insula in the Tiber the sacred serpent at once left the ship and found a refuge on the island. From that moment the plague is said to have rapidly disappeared.

In gratitude to the god, who was thus visibly among them in the serpent form, the south end of the island—perhaps, indeed, the whole of the island—was modelled into the shape of a great galley of hewn stone. A temple of Æsculapius (as the Romans called him) was built adjacent to it, with portico and abaton. A well existing there became sacred to Æsculapius, and from that day to this the

4

island in the Tiber has, through pagan and Christian times alike, been devoted to the cure and treatment of the sick. The stern of the stone galley still exists, with the effigy of the serpent and remains of the image of Æsculapius. The Church of St. Bartholomew stands on the site of the temple, and on, or near, the spot where stood the ancient abaton now stands a hospital served by the Brotherhood of San Juan de Dios, the benevolent saint of Granada, where the sick folk of Rome are helped and tended ; and there, unlike their predecessors of 2,200 years ago, if illness should terminate in death the poor weary souls are kindly and tenderly ministered to by priest, physician, and nurse, until they sink into the last sleep.

It is doubtless in consequence of this episode of the founding of a temple of Æsculapius on the island of the Tiber that the staff and serpent of the Epidaurian god have been, and remain to this day, the symbol of the profession of Medicine.

BIBLIOGRAPHY.

J. Baunack. Aus Epidauros, 1890 ; and Ἐφημερίς, 1884.

„ Zu den Inschriften am Epidauros. Philologus. 1895.

Ch. Blinkenberg. Inscriptions d'Epidaure. Nordisk Tidsskrift for Filologi. 1895.

P. Cavvadias. Πρακτικά τῇ Ἀρχαιολ. Ἐταιρίας. 1881, 82, 83, 84, etc.

„ Δελτίον ἀρχαιολογικόν. 1891.

„ Fouilles d'Epidaure. 1893.

„ Ἐφημερὶς Ἀρχαιολ. 1894.

Prof. Chipiez. Revue Archéolog. 1896.

Defrass & H. Lechat. Epidaure. 1895.

Ch. Diehl. Excursions Archéologiques en Grèce. 1890.

W. Dörpfeld. Berliner Philolog. Wochenschrift. 1890.

„ Athenische Mittheilungen. 1893.

„ Atike Denkmaeler, II, etc.

Dumon. Théâtre de Polyclète. 1889.

P. Foucart. Bulletin de Correspond. Hellénique. 1890.

Fraser's Pausanias. 1898.

Prof. A. Furtwängler, Berlin. Phil. Wochenschrift. 1888.

Gardner's New Chapters in Greek History.

P. Girard. L'Asklépieion d'Athènes. 1882.

S. Herlich. Epidaurus, eines Heilstätte. 1898.

Herold. Zeitschrift für Bauwesen. 1893.

G. Köhler. Athenische Mittheilungen. 1877.

Fr. Köpp. „ „ 1885.

C. H. Merriam. Marvellous Cures at Epidaurus. American Antiquarian, 1884.

C. H. Merriam. Dogs of Aesculapius. 1885.

S. Reinach. Revue Archéologique. 1884–85, etc.

M. Staïs. Ἐφημερίς. 1892, etc.

Alice Walton. Cult of Asklepios. Cornell Studies, No. III.

U. v. Wilamowitz-Möllendorff. Isyllos von Epidauros.

HERTFORD

PRINTED BY STEPHEN AUSTIN AND SONS.

www.ingramcontent.com/pod-product-compliance
Lightning Source LLC
Chambersburg PA
CBHW021235260626
47172CB00002B/783